The Crucifixi of Jesus

by

B.A.Ramsbottom

2002

Gospel Standard Trust Publications
12(b) Roundwood Lane
Harpenden
Hertfordshire
AL5 3DD
England

Published by:
Gospel Standard Trust Publications

2002

ISBN 1 897837 33 X

Printed by:
Dai Nippon Printing Co., (Hong Kong) Ltd.

The Upper Room

It is Jesus' last day. Tomorrow He is going to die. Often He had told His disciples that the time was coming when He must leave them and die—but they just did not seem to understand what He meant. We wonder why.

His last day was to be spent with His disciples. It was the Feast of the Passover—the time when the Jews remembered the lamb being killed, the blood sprinkled on the door, the angel of death passing over their houses. Year after year they remembered this. Now the time had come once again, and there were thousands of people who had come to Jerusalem to keep the Feast.

The Lord Jesus was going to keep the Feast with His disciples. So He sent two of them to get everything ready—the bread, the wine, the lamb. But first they needed somewhere to meet. So He sent two of them to find the place.

What do these two men keep looking for as they walk through the streets? Something strange —a man carrying a pot of water on his head. (Usually it would be only the women who did this.) Jesus had told them to look for this man, and then to go after him. At last they see him, and they do as they have been told.

The man goes into a house, so the two follow him in. "Where is the place where the Master shall keep the Passover?" they ask the owner of the house, and he kindly shows them the place. It is an upstairs room. He does not seem surprised. It is all ready. Jesus knows everything, and He knew just what this man would do and say.

Later Jesus and all His disciples gathered in this room and began to eat and drink. How happy they must have been! But no! Suddenly Jesus said, "One of you is going to betray Me to My enemies, who will kill Me."

The disciples were shocked. They looked at one another in sorrow. "Is it I?" one said. And then another, "Is it I?" Jesus said, "It is the one who shall dip his hand into the dish at the same time that I do."

The one who did so was called Judas Iscariot. He was one of Jesus' own disciples, but he did not love Him. He was a bad man, though the other disciples did not know this. He was a thief. He stole. And he wanted to get rid of Jesus. He had talked to Jesus' enemies and said, if they gave him some money, he would show them where Jesus was, so they could take Him and kill Him. How terrible!

Jesus was very, very sad. "What you are going

to do, do it quickly!" He said to Judas. And Judas went out, away from Jesus, into the darkness— for ever.

You can read about this in Matthew chapter 26, verses 17 to 25; Mark chapter 14, verses 12 to 21; Luke chapter 22, verses 7 to 18.

The Lord's Supper

But what is the Lord Jesus doing now? He is taking the bread from the table, and breaking it in pieces. He tells His disciples that just as the bread was being broken, soon His body would be broken on the cross. They were to eat the broken bread.

And what then? Jesus poured out the wine into a cup, and told them to drink it. He said that just as the wine was poured out, soon His blood would be poured out on the cross. How much He loved His disciples!

Jesus then said that, as long as the world lasts, His followers must meet and eat the broken bread and drink from the cup. We call it "the Lord's supper," and God's people still do this all over the world. Jesus said, "Do this in remembrance of Me." They are never to forget how much Jesus loved them when He died for them.

Afterwards they all sang a hymn and went out.

Then Jesus again told them something terrible. All of them would leave Him! You remember Peter? Peter was so upset that he cried out that if everyone else left his dear Lord and Master, he never would.

But Jesus answered: "Before the cock shall

crow tomorrow, Peter, during this very night, you will say you never knew Me."

Poor Peter thought this could not possibly happen. What? Deny Jesus? Never. But he did!

You can read about this in Matthew chapter 26, verses 26 to 32; Mark chapter 14, verses 22 to 26; Luke chapter 22, verses 19 and 20.

The Garden of Gethsemane

Jesus was now on His way to die. He knew that wicked people would seize Him and kill Him. But He was not afraid.

There was a garden just outside the stone walls of Jerusalem. It was close to the Mount of Olives. It was called the Garden of Gethsemane. It was a garden of olive trees. It was the place where Jesus loved to go and meet His friends and talk with them.

Here Jesus took Peter and James and John apart from the other disciples. But then He went a little further, telling them, "Stop here, and watch with Me."

The Lord Jesus was very, very sorrowful. A heavy weight was pressing on Him. He knew He must die, but it was not only that. He knew it would be a terrible death, not for Himself but for others—bearing all the dreadful weight of His people's sin. Not only would all His friends leave Him, but His own dear Father in heaven would turn away from Him.

It was a very, very bitter cup He must drink. "O Father," he prayed, "if it be possible, let this cup pass from Me," but then He said, "Nevertheless Thy will be done." So great was His agony and pain that great drops of blood poured from Him on to the ground.

Three times He came back to His disciples. Three times He found them asleep. Can you believe it? They had fallen fast asleep. Three times He prayed the same prayer. And then a holy angel came down from heaven to give Him strength. Though He was true, almighty God, He was also a real Man and needed strengthening.

At last He cried to His disciples, "Sleep on. Take your rest. The time has come. I am now going to be betrayed. Arise. Let us go."

O what love the Lord Jesus showed!

You can read about this in Matthew chapter 26, verses 36 to 46; Mark chapter 14, verses 32 to 42; Luke chapter 22, verses 39 to 46.

The Arrest

But what are all these lights? And who are all these people rushing forward through the darkness? They are armed. Some are carrying swords. Some spears. Some sticks. Some are soldiers. Some are priests.

And who is that at the front? It is the traitor Judas Iscariot. He is showing Jesus' enemies where they can find Him. And then he does a most awful, terrible thing! He kisses Jesus. He has told them that the one that he kisses is the one they must seize. "Judas," said the Lord Jesus, "betrayest thou Me with a kiss?"

The crowd surges forward. But Jesus does not run away. He goes to meet them. "Who are you seeking?" He asks.

"Jesus of Nazareth," they cry.

"I am He," calmly replies the Lord Jesus. And what do you think happened? At the sound of His almighty voice, they all fell back, helpless, on the ground.

Jesus showed them the power that He has because He is almighty God. Though He was going to die, He would teach them that it was not because He was weak. He would show them who He is. Did He not say, "No man can take My life

from Me. I have power to lay it down; and I have power to take it again"?

We again think of the wonderful love of Jesus. How easy for Him to escape!

Do you know the verse:

"It were an easy part
    For Him the cross to fly,
    But love to sinners fills His heart,
    And makes Him choose to die"?

You would have thought that now they all would have been so frightened that they would have fled away in terror. But no! Back they came. And Jesus asked them again, "Who are you seeking?" Again they said, "Jesus of Nazareth." But now Jesus gave Himself up into their wicked, cruel hands. "Take Me," He said, "but let these my followers go their way."

It is not surprising (is it?) that Peter was so angry that he drew his sword and attacked them. He even cut off one man's ear. But no! Jesus said, "Put your sword away, Peter. My Father has given Me this bitter cup to drink, and I am going to drink it." So Jesus made the man's ear better. That is how kind He is. Jesus did not need anybody to fight for Him with a sword. Had He asked, thousands of angels would have come down from heaven to fight for Him.

Then He let the soldiers tie Him up and take Him away.

You can read about this in Matthew chapter 26, verses 47 to 56; Mark chapter 14, verses 43 to 52; Luke chapter 22, verses 47 to 53; John chapter 18, verses 1 to 12.

"There was no other good enough
To pay the price of sin;
He only could unlock the gate
Of heaven, and let us in."

Jesus Before the High Priest

It is the middle of the night. All the city of Jerusalem is asleep as these wicked men hurry Jesus through the streets. They are on their way to the palace of Caiaphas. Caiaphas was the chief priest, but he was a bad man. He did not like Jesus.

But why did they treat Jesus so? What had He done that was wrong? Nothing. He had only been kind and done good. But the priests and rulers did not like Him because He told them about their bad ways.

At the high priest's palace, different people kept saying different things about Jesus—but they all disagreed with one another. At last they found two bad men who both told the same story—but it was not true.

Then the wicked priest Caiaphas had an idea. "Are you the Son of God?" he asked, and when Jesus said Yes, he said He must die. But why? Jesus IS the Son of God.

But what is happening now? Dreadful things! Some are spitting at Jesus, some are laughing at Him, some are hitting Him.

And down below in the courtyard was Peter. He had come along to see what would happen. You remember Peter? And what he had said? He would *never* deny his Lord and Master.

But see what is happening now. A girl says, "You are a follower of Jesus." Peter is frightened. They might capture him too. "No," he cries. "I am not."

Feeling cold, Peter goes to warm himself by a fire. Another girl asks him if he is one of Jesus' friends. Again Peter says, No—and he hurries away into the darkness where he cannot be seen.

But a few people are sure he is one of Jesus' disciples and say so. Now Peter gets very angry, and begins to shout, and tells them he never knew Jesus.

And what do you think happened then? What is that sound? A cock crowing. And Peter remembered what Jesus had told him. He looked up to where Jesus was being so cruelly treated—and Jesus was looking at him. What a sad, sad look!

Poor Peter was ashamed of himself. What had he done? He ran out and burst into tears. He was bitterly sorry.

But O that look! It condemned Peter. But it was a look of love. Jesus still loved him, and forgave him, even though he had done such a terrible thing.

You can read about this in Matthew chapter 26, verses 57 to 75; Mark chapter 14, verses 53 to 72; Luke chapter 22, verses 54 to 62; John chapter 18, verses 13 to 27.

"Behold the Man!"

Early in the morning there was another short meeting—to put Jesus to death. And again they mocked Him, and spit on Him, and hit Him. And again Jesus declared who He is—the Son of God.

Now Jesus is taken to the Roman ruler, Pilate. Why? Because the priests and Jewish rulers were not allowed to put Him to death, only the Romans.

It was to a magnificent palace that Jesus was rudely hurried through the crowded streets early that morning.

Pilate *knew* that Jesus had done nothing wrong, and said so—but he was frightened of the people. But see, who is this speaking to him now? It is his wife. She has had a terrible dream. She says, "Set Jesus free." But Pilate does not listen. He takes a bowl of water, and washes his hands. Why? He means, It is not my fault. Then he sends Jesus to Herod, the king of the Jews, but Herod sends Him back again to Pilate.

Then Pilate thinks of a good idea. In Jerusalem in prison is a terrible man. He is called Barabbas. He is a thief. He is a murderer. Pilate says to the people, "You can have one man free. Who would you like, Jesus or Barabbas?" And the people cry

Many girls and boys cannot understand *why* Jesus died. Why is there so much in the Bible about the cross? Why so much about Jesus dying? Why is it important? What has it got to do with people being forgiven? Why would no one have gone to heaven if Jesus had not been crucified?

God said all who do wrong must be punished. We have all done wrong and so we all deserve to be punished. But Jesus said He would be punished *instead* of His people—for their sins —so that they would not be punished.

That is why He was crucified. This is why He died.

> "He knew how wicked men had been;
> He knew that God must punish sin;
> So out of pity Jesus said
> He'd bear the punishment instead."

That is why the day when Jesus died is called Good Friday. All the good and gracious blessings God's people receive come through Jesus dying for them.

You can read about this in Matthew chapter 27, verses 31 to 35; Mark chapter 15, verses 21 and 22; Luke chapter 23, verses 26 to 31.

The Crucifixion

It was nine o'clock in the morning when Jesus was crucified. Over His head was a plaque: THIS IS JESUS THE KING OF THE JEWS. For six hours He hung, bleeding, dying on the cross.

At midday everything went dark. It was black like midnight—though this was springtime and the midday sun is usually very bright. It was as if the sun must hide itself when the Lord of all was dying.

Those around mocked: passers by, priests, soldiers; the soldiers even gambled as to who should have Jesus' coat. Someone offered Him a drink—but how bitter! It was vinegar.

Remember, Jesus had done nothing wrong, and how easily He could have escaped.

For most of the six hours Jesus was silent. Just seven times He spoke.

Once He spoke to John. You remember John? the youngest disciple that Jesus dearly loved. So kindly and lovingly Jesus looked on His sorrowful mother Mary, and told John to look after her.

For those who were being so cruel to Him, Jesus prayed. "Father, forgive them, they know not what they do."

Two thieves were crucified at the same time as Jesus, one on each side of Him. They were bad

men, and deserved to die. At first they both mocked Jesus.

But now what is happening? One of them is speaking. Listen! "We deserve to die, but this Man has done nothing wrong." How did this thief know that Jesus had done nothing wrong, that He was innocent? But now this thief is praying to Jesus. He calls Jesus LORD. He asks Him to remember him when He comes into His kingdom. He knows that Jesus is a King.

How did the dying thief learn all these things? That Jesus is a King? That He has a kingdom? That we can pray to Him? And that there is hope for a wicked man who has spent all his life in evil things? The Holy Spirit taught him these things in his heart.

But now listen to the Lord Jesus. What a wonderful, gracious word He now speaks! He tells the dying thief that this very day he will be with Him in heaven! This is what the Bible means when it speaks of "grace."

At last the Lord Jesus gave a shout: "IT IS FINISHED." All His sufferings and pains were finished, His life on earth was finished—but what did Jesus *really* mean? His great work of saving His people was now complete. Then He meekly bowed His head, and died.

Immediately there was a dreadful earthquake.

The earth shook, and even the rocks were broken in pieces. The one who had just died was the Lord of all, hills and fields and rocks and mountains. And now the earth itself must speak!

Yet the enemies of Jesus must have their last fling, and a cruel soldier plunged a spear into the side of Jesus. But another soldier, looking on His lifeless body, cried, "Truly this Man was the Son of God."

You can read about this in Matthew chapter 27, verses 33 to 56; Mark chapter 15, verses 23 to 41; Luke chapter 23, verses 32 to 49; John chapter 19, verses 16 to 37.

The Burial

It is now evening. The awful events of the day are over. The Sabbath will soon be here.

But who is this hurrying through the streets of Jerusalem? He is on his way to the Roman palace where Pilate is staying. He *must* see Pilate. He seems a very rich, important man. He is Joseph, known as Joseph of Arimathaea.

Boldly he goes in, and how surprised Pilate is! Joseph wants something very badly. He asks if he can have the body of Jesus so that it can be buried. And Pilate says, Yes.

Lovingly Joseph hurries back to Calvary. And there he sees another rich, important man approaching the cross. It is Nicodemus, who once came to Jesus by night because he was frightened. But like Joseph, he is frightened no longer. Like Joseph he cannot bear to think of the sacred body of the Lord Jesus being left on the cross—He must have a proper burial. And hundreds of years before God's prophet had said that so it would be.

Tenderly the two take down the body of Jesus and carry it to a nearby garden. Here was a grave that belonged to Joseph. It was like a cave, hewn out in the rock. Here they gently laid the lifeless body of Jesus. And they could not do enough. The pounds' worth of precious spices they had brought to anoint His body!

A great stone was rolled to the mouth of the grave. Later the rulers of the Jews knowing what had happened, sealed the stone and brought a guard of soldiers to keep watch—so no one could steal the body away.

Where are Peter and James and John and the others now? They have all fled. But silently watching are some of those women who loved Jesus so dearly.

* * *

There the body of Jesus lay in the cold, silent grave, quietly resting, His work finished. But it was impossible that Jesus could remain there. And so early in the morning on the third day there was an earthquake, a holy angel came down from heaven and rolled the stone away, and Jesus came forth out of the grave. He is alive again! He is the risen Saviour. He lives for ever. He was once crucified, but now He lives to die no more. He is the almighty Saviour.

You can read about this in Matthew chapter 27, verses 57 to 66; Mark chapter 15, verses 42 to 47, Luke chapter 23, verses 50 to 56; John chapter 19, verses 38 to 42. The chapters that follow tell how Jesus rose from the dead.